Marvin Behm

JOHN DEERE TRACTORS

Big green machines in review

Photography by Henry Rasmussen

Motorbooks International
Publishers & Wholesalers Inc

First published in 1987 by Motorbooks International Publishers & Wholesalers Inc, PO Box 2, 729 Prospect Avenue, Osceola, WI 54020 USA

© Henry Rasmussen, 1987
Reprinted spring 1993

Motorbooks International is a certified trademark, registered with the United States Patent Office

Printed in Hong Kong

The information in this book is true and complete to the best of our knowledge. All recommendations are made without any guarantee on the part of the author or publisher, who also disclaim any liability incurred in connection with the use of this data or specific details

We recognize that the name John Deere and the many tractor model names and designations are the property of Deere & Company. We use them to identify the products only. This is not an official publication of Deere & Company

Library of Congress Cataloging-in-Publication Data
Rasmussen, Henry
 John Deere tractors.

 1. John Deere tractors.
 2. Deere & Company—History.
I. Title.
TL233.5.R38 1987   629.2'25   86-33237
ISBN 0-87938-242-2

On the front cover, super-collector Lloyd Bellin of Isanti, Minnesota, high atop his 1953 GH. It was the largest John Deere of its time. This example is one of 237 units built, of which only a handful are known to exist today. On the back cover, 77-year-old Harold Bellin of Isanti, Minnesota, straddles the B he bought new from a local dealership in 1937. It has been restored by his grandson, and today stands every bit as clean and shiny as on the day of delivery.

Pictured on the half title, the rusty radiator of a 1930 GP. It resembles an overgrown historic marker—which it is, in a sense. Another monument of sorts is shown on the title page, a 1938 Model B sits abandoned on the endless prairie in South Dakota, left to die a slow death. The photograph on this page represents the versatility of the John Deere tractor. This styled B of prewar vintage has been set up to run a circular saw on a farm in Wisconsin.

CONTENTS

INTRODUCTION

A Man, An Idea, A Company

Yes, there is a man behind the corporate giant—a John Deere of flesh and blood, Or, there was. For John Deere, the man, died one hundred years ago. But before he died he had laid the foundation for an organization that would dominate its field and become one of the world's largest manufacturing companies in the process. Yet, it all began so humbly.

A native of Vermont, John Deere was born in 1804. After only the most rudimentary schooling, he took a job with a blacksmith in Rutland. When the four-year apprenticeship came to an end, he set up his own shop, and soon became known in the local area for his well-crafted hayforks and shovels. Already then, there was something special about his products—in addition to their high quality, their metal parts were always polished, a feature that would soon reveal its significance.

When a depression hit Vermont, John Deere, like so many other New Englanders, decided to try his luck in the new frontier—out west. After a journey that required the use of a stagecoach as well as a variety of boats, he arrived in Grand Detour, Illinois, in 1836. Among the settlers of this small community, located on the shore of the Rock River, there was such a demand for his services that after only a few days he was in full swing at the anvil.

But he soon found that the farmers faced a serious problem. The cast-iron plows they had brought from New England, where the ground had been light and sandy, did not work well here. The rich midwestern soil had a tendency to stick to the mold board, so that it had to be scraped clean with frustrating frequency. Many farmers were so discouraged that they considered moving on. But John Deere soon had a solution.

Using the broken piece of a mill blade, he fashioned the first-ever steel plow. Its advantages lay in the curve of the mold board, and in the fact that its surface was highly polished. A well-attended test was staged on a local farm, and the new steel plow was found to work beautifully.

But John Deere was more than just a clever blacksmith. He understood the virtues of mass production and mass marketing. Instead of building to order, he built up a stock, then took to the road, visiting the farmers in the field, demonstrating his revolutionary "self-polisher."

What had begun as a one-man operation, soon required larger facilities, as well as a location better situated in relation to established transport routes. So the company moved to Moline, Illinois. It was also at this time that John Deere persuaded a Pittsburg mill to roll the special steel needed for his product. By 1847, the company was well on its way to success, producing 1,000 plows a year.

John Deere was a big man, stern-faced and strong. But if he was strong, he was also strong-willed. And he was not a man of many words. He is even said to have been somewhat gruff. Yet, he possessed qualities that have left their indelible imprint on the company. Honesty and integrity were key characteristics, along with his genuine concern for the farmers and their needs, his unyielding commitment to quality, and his strong belief in the necessity of constantly improving the product.

A contributing factor in the successful propagation of these beliefs is the fact that the company has always been led by a member of the Deere family. Several years before his death in 1886, John Deere was succeeded by his son, Charles Deere. The establishing and nurturing of a distribution network, crucial to the future success of the company, is contributed to him, as is the development of several new product lines. At his death in 1907, the organization manufactured a large variety of steel plows, as well as planters and cultivators.

William Butterworth, Charles' son-in-law, added to the full-service nature of the company by buying up a number of related producers of farm equipment. A move that would prove to be of special significance was the 1918 purchase of the Waterloo Gasoline Traction Engine Company, manufacturer of the first tractor to carry the John Deere name.

Charles Deere Wiman, John's grandson, took over in 1928. In 1937, coinciding with the company's centennial celebration, John Deere reached a gross sales figure of one hundred million dollars. And before his death in 1955, Wiman had the satisfaction of seeing the company enter the select group of the one hundred largest corporations in the world.

Wiman's son-in-law, and successor, William Hewitt, brought the company to the point where it is today. More than six hundred different products are now found in the John Deere catalog. Many of these are manufactured outside the United States. There are plants in twelve countries, located on four continents. Furthermore, this multitude of merchandise is distributed in more than one hundred markets around the world. The organization counts approximately 50,000 people on its payroll, and the annual sales figure has passed the five-billion-dollar mark.

The Deere company is exceptionally well set for the future, with its products in the forefront of the field. The caretakers of the John Deere heritage have indeed been faithful to the principles of their founding father. "If we do not improve our plows, someone else will, and we shall lose our trade," John Deere is quoted as once having said.

It is of some significance, although certainly a coincidence, that the universally known company symbol, the deer, captures the graceful animal moving forward with giant strides—something John Deere, the man, would have liked.

Progenitor of a proud line

In the beginning there was no Deere; that is, the first Deere was not truly a Deere. In 1892, an Iowa engineer by the name of John Froehlich developed the first gasoline tractor able to propel itself both forward and backward. But it proved no great success. Unperturbed, Froehlich went on to form the Waterloo Gasoline Traction Engine Company, through which his experiments led to improved versions.

However, these models were still not marketable. The world had to wait until 1912 to see the first commercially successful tractor produced by the company. It was called the Waterloo Boy.

In Moline, Illinois, John Deere had also experimented with tractors, but had not been successful in developing a suitable design. Seeing a solution in the Waterloo Boy, John Deere purchased the company and continued production of its tractor until the first genuine, all-Deere model was introduced in 1923.

This photograph of a 1916 Model R Waterloo Boy shows the machinery in all its exposed simplicity. The engine is located on the left side of the vehicle, with the head of the horizontal two-cylinder unit (note the two spark plugs) facing the operator. On the right side one can see the flywheel and the gears of the single-speed transmission. The red caps are the covers of the grease cups.

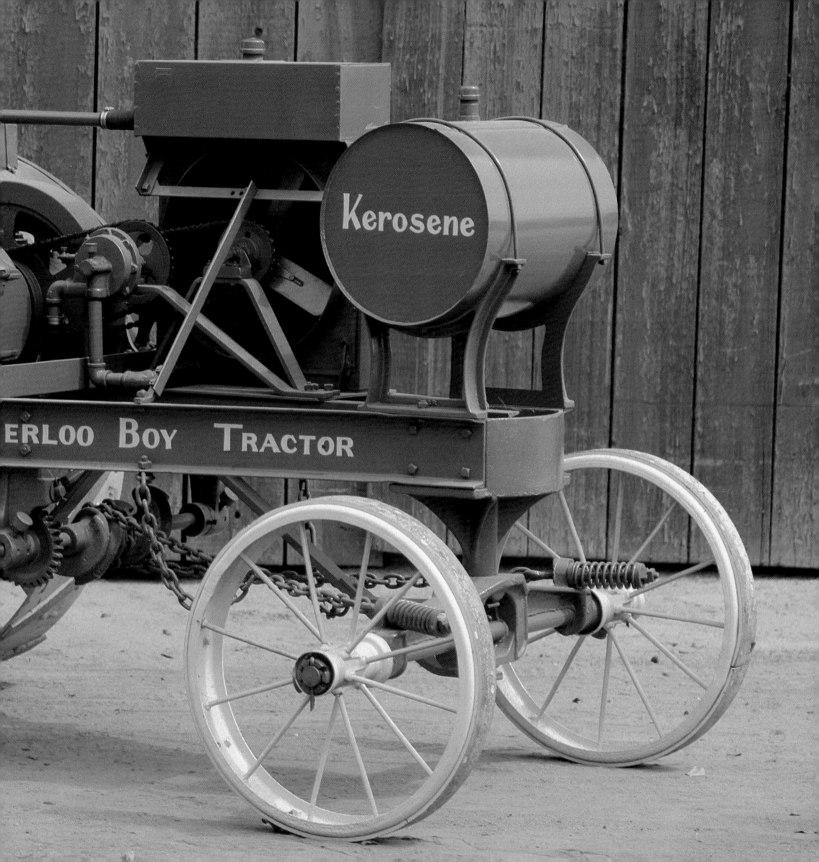

Previous page
The superbly restored Model R
Waterloo Boy featured on the
previous pages was
manufactured in 1916. Its serial
number is 1523, and it spent most
of its long life in Colorado
Springs, Colorado. When found,
it was in restorable condition with
the original green paint remaining
in places. The only parts missing
were the fuel tank and the
radiator. The restoration is the
work of owner Bert Ballatore, of
Ripon, California. It occupied ten
years of his spare time.

Pictured on this spread is another
1916 Model R Waterloo Boy. This
unit is considered one of the best
preserved original examples of its
type. Note that the gas tank is set
on its end, a feature thought to
have been unique to a limited
number of Waterloo Boys. Still
debating whether to restore it or
not, owner Don Dufner of Buxton,
North Dakota, enjoys an
occasional jaunt with this
progenitor of all Deere tractors,
which still runs, producing a most
impressive thunder.

The photographs on this spread offer an interesting comparison between the restored and unrestored rear wheels of two Waterloo Boys. The restorer was careful to leave the original spokes in place, even if it meant allowing some pitting to show through the paint. Notice the three struts that keep the wheel from separating from the final-drive gear.

The Waterloo Boy came in three basic versions: the L, the most rare (only 29 units were built); the R; and the most common, the N. Altogether some 30,000 units were manufactured between 1914 and 1924. All had chain steering until 1920, and all had the two-cylinder engine. The L and R versions featured one speed only, while the N sported a two-speed transmission.

The firstborn offspring

After Deere's 1918 takeover of the Waterloo organization, the combined engineering staff members spent their first years improving the Waterloo Boy. In 1921, they began drawing up plans for an all-new tractor, a creation that would have a profound effect on the productivity of the American farmer, a product that would put the John Deere name on the map as one of the world's foremost tractor manufacturers. This was the beloved Model D, introduced in 1923.

The machine had now taken on the shape we perceive a tractor should have: the engine located in the center and the radiator positioned in front of it. The engine was new, but still of the two-cylinder, horizontal design. Simple and rugged construction made it extremely durable. While the Waterloo Boy produced 12 hp at the drawbar, the original D was rated at 15 hp.

During its life span, which was longer than any other tractor's, it was continuously improved. When the last D rolled off the line in 1953, almost 200,000 units had been built.

The owner of this charming contraption, Charles Morgantini of Greenfield, California, is not sure of its exact vintage. The D has been sitting by the entrance of the farm for so many years that he has forgotten. The manufacturer's plate is unreadable, painted over and overgrown with weeds. But, judging from the style of the air cleaner, as well as the fact that the machine does not roll on rubber, the old workhorse is most likely from the early thirties.

Pictured on these pages is another gem from the Morgantini farm. This survivor is of 1929 vintage. Missing from the rear wheels of the D are the ingenious cleats of pressed steel. Also missing are the metal bands usually attached to the front wheels (rubber tires did not become available until the mid-thirties). Note the JD logo molded into the center of the rear wheel.

Shown here are details of an unusually well preserved Model D from 1925. It was found on the Dufner farm in North Dakota. The perforated steering wheel, which is located to the left of center, is peculiar to the earlier D models. Close scrutiny of the transmission cover shows it to carry the inscription, "Waterloo Gasoline Engine Co. Waterloo Iowa, U.S.A." While the paint is most likely of a second or third generation, the wood in the operator's platform is certainly original.

The photograph above focuses attention on the flywheel. The first 880 units were introduced with a spoked unit of 26 inch diameter. On this example from 1925, the flywheel is still spoked, but its diameter has been reduced by two inches. Soon after, it became solid, the obvious reason being the great danger posed by the spinning contraption. The D had only two forward speeds. Final drive was of a roller-chain construction, a design unchanged during the entire production run.

A passion for machinery

Bert Ballatore's parents came over from Italy in the late teens. They settled in California's San Joaquin Valley, where they planted almonds and grapes. A variety of mechanical equipment was always to be found on the farm, and young Bert grew up in the tradition of love and respect for the machines that simplified the cultivation of the soil.

Later in life, when he had taken over responsibility for the farm, he found himself becoming interested in the preservation of this equipment, especially plows to begin with. In the mid-sixties he acquired a John Deere Model D, and proceeded to refurbish it from the ground up.

Finding that he enjoyed tinkering with these old machines—they were projects well suited for the periods of leisure that come and go with the seasons on the farm—he proceeded to look for a Waterloo Boy, which he finally located. Today, his collection, which he humbly does not refer to as a collection, consists of fourteen restored and unrestored John Deere tractors.

In this photograph, Bert Ballatore attends to the needs of his exquisitely restored Waterloo Boy. The rocker arms have to be oiled periodically. An oil can is permanently placed on the vehicle for this purpose, since periodically does not mean every other month, but every other hour or so that it is driven across the field. This is one of the many chores that keep the operator from getting bored.

In the picture to the left Bert
Ballatore exercises the first of his
restoration projects, a Model D
from 1928, chassis number 54654.
This survivor belonged to a
neighbor, who was the original
owner and who, toward the end
of the tractor's life, relegated it to
the duty of running a pump. This
early D did not originally come
with rubber wheels. It was,
however, a very common
conversion that most owners
made as soon as it became
available.

In the photograph above, Bert
Ballatore and a friend chat about
the steering wheel from
Ballatore's 820 Deere. During a
scraping operation many years
ago, the scraper bucket broke
and fell back across the top of the
tractor, putting the steering wheel
out of commission—but
fortunately not the driver. Next on
Ballatore's list of restoration
projects is a very early Model D,
number 31 off the production
line.

What cannot be seen in this photograph are the almond trees that surround the old corrugated tin building on Bert Ballatore's 90 acre spread. The trees are the reason the setting is well suited for his 1935 GPO (the O stands for orchard). This unrestored workhorse came from neighboring Escalon, California, where it also served in an almond orchard. Note that the exhaust pipe cannot be seen from this angle. It is located on the other side of the engine, and protrudes horizontally so as not to interfere with leaves and fruit hanging from the branches.

Arrival of a do-all descendant

Tractor technology progressed rapidly in the twenties, and the Deere engineers soon came up with a creation that was more useful than the Model D (not that this affected the sales of the D to a noticeable degree). The popularity of the original Deere was unshakable. The older machine was stronger than the new one and still well suited for the task of pulling large farm implements across the field. But the fitting of a power lift which raised and lowered equipment such as planters and cultivators, a first in the industry, gave the new GP, introduced in 1928, greater versatility.

GP stood for general purpose, a designation describing the new machine well. Another feature that added greatly to the usefulness of the GP was its arched front axle. This allowed greater clearance for row-crop work.

The two-cylinder engine, still horizontal, produced 10 hp at the drawbar. The GP was discontinued in 1935, after about 30,000 of the standard version had been built.

Shown here against the backdrop of out-of-commission Deeres is a perfectly restored GP, dating from 1928. It belongs to Lloyd Bellin of Isanti, Minnesota, and is an example of not only the quality but the uniqueness of his collection. To be perfectly correct, this splendid survivor is actually one of the first 110 GPs built. At that point, they were designated Model C. Those Cs were later recalled to the factory for GP modification.

In some cases, it is difficult to decide when to restore and when not to, since some of the nostalgic charm is always lost in the process of making the machinery look new again. This 1928 GP, captured in its natural environment, complete with barnyard, weathered fence, green grass and yellow dandelions (the rusty metal blends perfectly with this setting), exemplifies the point. Its owner, Lester Rydeen of Marine on St. Croix, Minnesota, has not made up his mind yet.

This close-up of the operator's workplace shows that Rydeen's GP is still complete, down to the last detail. With such simple and rugged construction, it is hard to imagine that anything would ever break. The steering wheel, with its delicately tapered and curved spokes, is peculiar to the GP. Note the gated gearshift lever in the center, below the steering wheel. Protruding to the right is the long clutch lever.

Previous page
Peering out the window of the old barn on the farm where he grew up (as shown in the photograph on the previous spread), Lester Rydeen takes in the rear view of another of his GPs, this particular example dating from 1929. At first sight the paint looks original, which would be quite unusual for such an old tractor. But a closer examination shows that a coat of green has indeed been applied on top of the old coat.

From the beginning all the way up to 1960, all Deeres were powered by the horizontal two-cylinder engine. The photograph above shows the simplicity of it all. This simplicity greatly contributed to the dependability of the Deere product, and also made it easier for the farmers to make necessary repairs. The engine operated at 950 rpm, and was started by simply cranking the flywheel.

The photograph to the right shows the great advantage of the GP model: its arched front axle. To accomplish increased clearance in the rear as well, the final drive was moved from the center of the axle to the outer ends. This feature made the GP the perfect machine for row-crop work, where it would straddle one row, and work three. For still greater versatility, a third gear was added.

The year 1929 saw the introduction of a special version of the GP, the Wide-Tread. Its advantage was that, thanks to a longer rear axle, it could straddle two rows, with the narrow front wheels fitting between the rows. This was the first Deere tricycle design. Cotton growers were particularly thrilled with this new versatility. In this picture from the Bellin collection in Minnesota, a restored 1931 Wide-Tread follows an unrestored unit from 1930. Note the self-cleaning wheels on the restored tractor.

A big brother with winning ways

Anew heir to the Deere legacy arrived in 1934, with the introduction of the big Model A. The increase of the drawbar output to 16 hp was an almost unimportant feature compared to the great advantage of the many other innovations. The fact that the rear wheels were sliding and could be adjusted to any row width meant much greater versatility. In addition, a new one-piece transmission case allowed still higher clearance. These features were both industry firsts.

Another improvement was that the power shaft and the implement hitch had been relocated to the center of the tractor, which took care of the side-draft problem. Yet another improvement was that the power lift was no longer mechanical but hydraulic, which meant greater ease of operation as well as a cushioned drop when the equipment was lowered.

The A remained in production until 1952. Approximately 300,000 units were manufactured, making the A the best-selling tractor in the company's history.

Here's testimony to the great longevity of Deere machinery. This A was built in 1936; 50 years later, the tractor is still going strong. The secret, of course, lies not only in its simple and rugged construction, but in the owner's ability to keep the machine running. This scene is in North Dakota, where the size alone of the fields guarantees the tractors get a thorough workout. There is no telling how many hours of operation this old workhorse has seen.

Featured here is another unique tractor from the Bellin collection. This one is also a Model A (an AOS actually, the O standing for orchard, the S for streamlined). The concept of providing a special version for orchard use was introduced earlier with the GP. Some of these As had fenders that were completely skirted, which prevented branches from catching in the spokes. This AOS is from 1937, and one of approximately 800 built.

To the left is another view of the AOS, showing off its elegantly streamlined cowling and fenders. The low position of the seat (note the ingenious spring suspension) and the steering wheel allowed the driver to operate the tractor from a vantage point where he was able to avoid most of the branches. It is difficult to find orchard tractors in good condition, due to the fact that the metal panels get pitted from the chemicals used for spraying.

Shown in the picture above is an A of 1938 vintage. But this is no ordinary A, it is an ANH (the N denoting narrow, and H standing for high). This particular example is one of only 26 units made during a period when the Deere engineers experimented with new applications for their products. Note the early use of a single wheel up front. Lloyd Bellin is behind the controls of this unique machine which was originally found on a farm in Arizona.

A virtuous smaller twin

There seemed to be no backwater in the stream of new creations that flowed from John Deere's busy engineering department. Those at the drawing boards were kept on their toes by the marketing people, who were in close contact with the dealers, who in turn communicated directly with the farmers. This chain of communication was activated after the introduction of the A, which was the largest Deere of its time. Its versatility brought tractor technology forward with leaps and bounds. But then, farmers who cultivated smaller fields and crops began asking for a smaller tractor—one that offered all the innovations of the A.

The Model B was that smaller twin. It was introduced in 1935, and was literally an A scaled down one-third in size and power. It had all the features of the A, such as adjustable wheel tread, hydraulic power lift and four-speed transmission. But power was only 9 hp, which meant lower operating costs.

The photograph on this spread features a B half-buried in the tall grass on a Minnesota farm. Without an A by its side, it is difficult to tell it apart from its larger twin. On the following spread, a beautifully restored B rests on the freshly cut lawn of the Bellin farm. Notice how the wheels, both front and rear, have been set back to their narrowest adjustment point, which is the way it ran during its tour of duty in a vineyard in northern California. This example is of 1938 vintage.

All in the family

It is not unusual to encounter a farming family in which each generation has been involved with John Deere machinery. As profound an impact as the green and yellow tractors have had in the field of agriculture in this country and all over the world, it would be nearly impossible for this *not* to happen. But it is unusual to find a family in which the daily lives of all four generations have evolved and will continue to evolve around things Deere as have the Bellins of Isanti, Minnesota.

Great-grandfather Harold Bellin bought his first Deere in 1937, and farmed his land with this faithful servant, and subsequent ones, for decades. Grandfather Lloyd collects them on a grand scale (one would be hard pressed to find a finer and more complete collection anywhere); father Mike restores them full time; and son Colt plays with them, also full time.

This photograph captures the essence of Harold Bellin. He is a humble, honest, hard-working man of habit, whose interests center around the land, the crop and the family. His face reflects the life of a farmer—hard at times but toughening, happy at times and quite soothing. The clothes, the barn, the machine are all part of the environment he knows best and loves most. At the age of 77, even the act of peering into the tank has become habit.

51

Harold Bellin still remembers the day in 1937 when he drove his brand-new John Deere Model B home from the dealership in Weber, Minnesota. He paid $740 for it; that included a plow. The tractor did the work he had needed five horses to do before. Son Lloyd learned to operate it when he was seven. Now the old iron horse has been restored by grandson Mike.

Previous page
On the previous spread, photographed in front of one of the barns that house the Bellin collection, are the smallest and the largest members of the Deere dynasty at that time. The small machine is a Model 62 from 1937. This example is one of only 79 built. It was the forerunner of the Model L, introduced later that year. The L was Deere's first utility tractor. It was also the first to feature a vertical two-cylinder engine. This little machine had a rating of 7 hp at the drawbar.

Featured to the right is a different view of the largest of the Deeres up until 1953. Lloyd Bellin, straddling this 1953 Model G, is dwarfed by the giant, whose 20 hp measured at the drawbar could handle three 14 inch plows, or ten-foot single disks, or three-row bedders. The size of this particular example is exaggerated by the fact that it is one of the unusual high-crop versions, a GH model. Only half a dozen are known to exist today.

To the left, Lloyd Bellin stands beside one of the jewels of his collection, the very first unit of the styled B to come off the production line. The serial number is 60000, the production year is 1939. The odds of finding such a gem are one in a million. Coincidence led Bellin to it on a farm in western Wisconsin. Another of Bellin's jewels is his wife Annette, seated on the tractor. She shares her husband's interests and handles the machinery nearly as proficiently.

Pictured above, two-year-old Colt practicing row-crop work on the Bellin farm. The tractor is from 1950, and was the first pedal-type toy to emulate a Deere. It was perfect for smaller fields, and at its best when the rows were very narrow and the crop very young. However, as the plants grew taller, especially when the crop consisted of corn, the model's usefulness was greatly reduced by its tendency to become lost in the field. Power output varied greatly from operator to operator.

Growing up and shaping up

The first three decades of tractor development were chiefly concerned with the technical aspects of the product. The tractor was, after all, just a utilitarian vehicle; as long as it performed its task to the satisfaction of the farmer, its appearance did not matter a whole lot.

Then, with increased interest in industrial design, a trend began conquering the nation in the late twenties and early thirties, giving new shape to everything from toasters to typewriters. Tractors, too, began to receive the magic touch. It was a matter of survival, a means of competition, for it was the consensus of the buying public that if a product *looked* good, it must also *be* good.

Deere retained one of the foremost designers in the field, Henry Dreyfuss, to perform this magic. The result was first seen in 1938, with the restyling of the A and B models. The new look was then applied to the D in 1939, the G in 1942 and subsequently to all new tractors.

Pictured here is a B from 1941. In collector terminology, a tractor with this new look is referred to as "styled," while a tractor manufactured before this period is called "unstyled." Besides giving the new tractors a modern appearance, the new look also strengthened the uniform image of Deere, a task that up until then had been left to the green and yellow paint.

Manufactured between 1939 and 1947, the HN (the N denoted that the tractor was fitted with a single front wheel) was quite a small tractor, somewhere between the LA and the B models in size and power. Both were replaced by the M. The H was the perfect tractor for the smaller farm or the farm with lighter chores (such as the orchard).

Bert Ballatore's almond orchard in Ripon, California. He bought two examples of the H many years ago, paying just $100 for each. One is still being used for cutting hay. The other, the one featured here, has been retired, at least for now. Note the narrow tread in the picture above. The H still used the two-cylinder horizontal engine, as seen in the picture to the left. The drawbar rating was 9 hp. It was the last model to be released before the outbreak of World War II.

No new tractors were introduced during the war, only variations of existing models. Then, in 1947, came the first postwar release. It was the M, a small utility-type tractor, producing 14 hp at the drawbar. The M sported many of the innovations the engineers had recently introduced on the older models, as well as a feature of its own, called Touch-O-Matic. This innovation employed hydraulics to simplify the attaching and controlling of equipment.

The photograph on this spread
shows a 1949 Model M as used by
Ballatore for various chores in his
vineyard. Ballatore runs a fleet of
M models, purchased secondhand
for around $300 each. The side
view shows that the engineers had
begun the switch to a vertical
engine. Notice also the orchard-type
exhaust. The M was the first model
to be built at the new Deere factory
in Dubuque, Iowa.

The head of a new generation

When studying the genealogy of Deere, it is helpful to organize its members into generations. The easiest way to determine the break between one generation and another is to judge the offspring by their appearance.

The first generation began with the D, introduced in 1923. For more than a decade the tractors looked basically the same, with the radiator and the steering mechanism exposed.

Then, with the advent of the styled tractors in the late thirties, the second generation arrived. This generation lasted about a decade, until the new look of the late forties. This was the beginning of the third generation.

It seems perhaps unfair to disregard technical advances when grouping generations, but in the case of the third generation, the visual and mechanical came together in one giant advancement: the introduction of diesel power. The first model powered by this new engine was the Model R.

The R replaced the aging D, which had been designed mainly for service on the larger farms of the nation's wheatland. The D had gradually received more power, 24 hp in 1935 and 30 hp in 1940. With the arrival of the R, Deere's largest tractor had a drawbar output of 34 hp. This picture shows an R at work in its favorite environment, one where the sky is big, the fields large, the loads heavy and the runs long.

The restyling of the new-generation Deere tractors did not only mean that the slots of the grille became vertical instead of horizontal; there was also more use of yellow paint. A band of the classic Deere color framed the upper and forward edges of the engine compartment. Also introduced were rear wheel fenders as well as a housing to cover the flywheel. Elvin Dammann is behind the controls of an aging 1952 Model R, owned by Larry Levin, Chisago Lakes, Minnesota.

To the right, an original 1949 R awaits its turn to be restored for the Bellin collection in Minnesota. Note that the new diesel engine still followed the old horizontal two-cylinder theme that had been with Deere since the days of the Waterloo Boy. The Model R was the first Deere with an optional steel cab. The one in this picture, however, is not a factory job. The dealer sign above the door of the workshop is from the late twenties.

In 1952, the A and B models were replaced by the 60 and 50. The following year brought the 70, a replacement for the G. Pictured here is a 1954 model from the Dufner farm in North Dakota. This version was the first diesel-powered row-crop Deere. A V-4 gasoline engine was employed for starting; power at the drawbar was 34 hp. The 70 diesel set a new fuel-economy record for row-crop tractors, and was also the first such tractor to come equipped with power steering as a factory option.

Featured on this spread are two of the smaller type of tractors from the middle and late fifties, both found at the Dufner Farm. Pictured to the left is a standard-version 320. This model was introduced in 1956, and also came in a lower-profile utility version. The 320 replaced the 40, which had replaced the M. Like the bigger tractors in the 20-series, this smaller one came with a three-point hitch, Touch-O-Matic hydraulics and independent disc brakes.

Pictured above is the 330, a 1958 replacement for the 320. The major differences came about as a result of restyling and re-engineering the driver comfort area (incorporated on the entire 30-series). There was a new, slanted instrument panel, adjustable deep-cushioned seat and angled steering wheel. The 330 came only with a gasoline engine, and had a four-speed transmission. Power at the drawbar was about 17 hp. The model was replaced in 1960 by the new-generation 1010.

Previous page
Featured on the previous spread, as well as on these pages, is the high-crop version of the 420, in this case fitted with the wide-axle front. The 420, introduced in 1956 and built until 1958, was one of the most versatile small tractors ever marketed by John Deere. It could be had in just about any configuration. Besides the Hi-Crop, there was the Standard, the Utility and the Special, the latter sporting a 27 inch clearance and a wide range of wheel spacings. Drawbar power for all versions was 20 hp.

The photograph above shows the workplace of the 420. The throttle lever is located just ahead of the steering wheel. The two small gauges are oil pressure and amp meters, while the large one is a combined tachometer and hour counter. The switch below this gauge controls the ignition, as well as the dim and bright lights. The starter knob is located on the right-hand side, the choke on the left. The clutch is foot operated and located on the left side, while the brake pedals are both found on the right-hand side.

The clearance of the high-crop version is 32 inches, which fits the bill perfectly for the farmer of these fields north of King City, California, where the main crop is tomatoes. The rear view shows the Touch-O-Matic hydraulic system. Notice that the farmer is not beyond making his own innovative improvements of the Deere's seating comfort. He has installed a backrest that looks as if it might have come from a discarded office chair.

Shown on this spread is a 420 Standard with single-wheel front end. It is set up for row-crop work and has an 80 inch rear wheel tread. The crops on this Greenfield, California, farm are mainly lettuce, broccoli and beets. In this configuration the tractor cultivates four rows per pass. This old workhorse is owned by Charles Morgantini, of Swiss and Italian heritage, whose father (still going strong at age 90) bought the tractor new in 1956, and the farm in 1935. Morgantini is an avid collector of tractors and other farm machinery. A small portion of his fleet is seen in the background.

81

Previous page
In 1956, a major engineering
effort produced the 20-series and
its 520, 620 and 720 variations,
effectively replacing the 50, 60
and 70 models. The picture on
this spread, photographed in
front of a corn grower's barn in
Minnesota, features a 720 from the
introductory year. The 20-series
had all-new engines, still of the
horizontal two-cylinder
configuration, but with improved
cylinder head and pistons that
increased combustion-chamber
turbulence and power. The 720
had a drawbar rating of 40 hp.

A host of innovations graced the
20-series, including Custom
Powr-Trol, which enabled the
operator to preset working
depths, and Load-and-Depth
Control, which kept the
implement working at a uniform
depth regardless of variations in
ground condition. Further
engineering efforts in the area of
driver comfort resulted in the
Float-Ride seat, which adjusted to
fit the driver, and effectively
smoothed the movements of a
rough ride.

The 820 was a hunk of a tractor, the largest and most powerful Deere of its time. This heavy-duty machine was built in the diesel tradition, as pioneered by the Model R and its successor, the 46 hp 80, but its engine had been increased to produce as much as 52 hp at the drawbar. The 820 shown in the photograph to the right, still in use on a farm in California's fertile San Joaquin Valley, dates from 1958, its last year of production.

Next page
The successor to the 820, the 830, was built between 1958 and 1961. It was even bigger than its predecessor, and weighed more than four tons. Innovations included a choice of starting systems: a V-4 gasoline engine or a convenient all-electric battery-operated arrangement. A foot-operated throttle was another option. The 830 pictured on the following spread, of 1960 vintage, is the newest component of an old fleet of Deeres that still provides the sole source of tractor power on a North Dakota farm.

This 630 of nonspecific vintage was photographed on a farm in South Dakota. The old workhorse has just one duty nowadays, easing its owner's job of transporting feed to the cattle. In its day, the 630 perfectly met the needs of medium and large farms, where its power could handle four-bottom plows and six-row planters. The larger tractors in the 30-series all had six-speed transmissions, which further improved their ability to handle tough assignments.

Next page

The example of a 1960 Model 435 featured on the following spread represents the ultimate development of the 30-series. Fitted on this tractor are the new-style fenders, which featured dual, sealed-beam headlights mounted below the forward edges. Seen in action on a North Dakota farm, the 435 is utilizing its PTO (power take-off) of either 540 rpm or 1000 rpm to perform the duty of cutting and crimping hay. Drawbar rating was 29 hp.

The old-fashioned farmer

The words "old fashioned" can carry a negative connotation. In this case, they do not. When an old-fashioned farmer like Don Dufner of Buxton, North Dakota, can stay on his land and make a decent living, the meaning is positive. Dufner's formula for success is found in the fact that he uses old machinery. He owns hundreds of old Deeres. Most of them dot the landscape around the barns, but many are on active duty.

The oldest tractor in use is from the early thirties; the newest is from the late fifties. These old workhorses have been purchased at auctions for next to nothing. In this way Dufner, first of all, does not have to make payments and, second, he can afford to use a different tractor for each chore and implement, meaning increased convenience.

If the old machinery breaks, he probably owns a backup; if not, he repairs it. If the old machinery is out of date, he builds his own; if that doesn't work—well, that hasn't happened yet.

Don Dufner bought this 1937 Model B longer ago than he can remember. But he does remember that his wife had won $35 at a tractor pull that day. At the same fair, there was an implement auction. The Dufners thought they could use the B, so they put up the winnings, added another $30, and drove it home. Now the B is permanently hooked up to the manure spreader. It too is from the thirties.

Pictured to the left is Don Dufner—old-fashioned farmer, master mechanic and Deere devotee—cheerfully displaying the workings of one of his several Waterloo Boys. Pictured above is an example of the improvizations his ingenious mind and nimble fingers have produced. The 830 needed more traction, so what more obvious solution than adding another pair of wheels and utilizing a coupling device of his own construction?

Next page
The contraption on the following spread is another example of Dufner's dexterity. The object here was to create the perfect setup for eight-row bean cultivation. Dufner added to this mid-forties Model G a pair of rear wheels located on axle extensions to fit the rows. Also added was a longer front axle, moved forward to make room for the cultivator, which was originally a 12-row sugar beet unit. An exhaust-pipe extension keeps the fumes away from the driver, and a spotlight gives him night vision.

Revolution in the old ranks

In 1953, a team of Deere engineers was given the assignment to create a new generation of tractors. Engine, chassis, transmission and hydraulics experts were all part of the team. To keep their efforts under wraps and also create ideal conditions, the team worked in a separate building. The results of this ambitious effort were not seen until 1960, with the introduction of an all-new line. It was the most revolutionary event in John Deere tractor history since the introduction of the first model in 1923.

With the new line, the days of the two-cylinder were finally over. Larger farms, demands for more power and speed and new fuels were the combined factors that forced the demise of the classic Deere engine. The first four tractors of this new generation were the 1010, the 2010, the 3010 and the 4010—creations that had a profound impact on tractor technology as well as on farming as a whole.

The photograph on this spread focuses on one of the most revolutionary elements of Deere's new tractor line, the engine. Massive intake manifold and curling exhaust header make the tractor engine look more like that of a sports car. This already fading workhorse is a Model 5020, built between 1965 and 1972. Its six-cylinder engine, with its cylinders arranged vertically, produced 116 hp at the drawbar, which made it the most powerful tractor of its time.

The photograph on this spread shows the full figure of the classic sixties Deere, the 5020. Its predecessor, the 5010, introduced in 1962, was the first addition to the fourth-generation Deeres, and was also the first two-wheel tractor to break the 100 hp barrier. With the 5020, even more power was available. The styling of this generation of tractors was striking. Note the new front, with its sharklike visage, new radiator grilles (one on each side of the body) and new instrument console.

Next page
Featured on the following spread is another Deere classic from the late sixties, the 4020, the most popular tractor of its time. What the D and A models had meant to the first generation, and the H and M to the second generation, the 4020 meant to the fourth generation. Nearly 200,000 units were sold. The third generation did not produce figures near these. However, the best sales performers of that era were the 70 and 420 models.

Previous page
The 3010 was one of the four tractors of the new fourth generation introduced in 1960. This workhorse from 1962 has seen hard labor on a farm in Greenfield, California, and yet the engine has been overhauled only once. Here it is set up for cultivating beets, lettuce and broccoli. The two cultivating bars are fitted with appropriate knives and gauge wheels, and cover eight rows per pass. The 3010 was built between 1960 and 1963, and had a rating of 54 hp.

This was the giant of the new generation. The 7520 reflected the three proven methods for increased traction and efficiency: adding weight and wheels and four-wheel drive. Of course, with this came an increase in power as well. The engine of this massive machine (turbocharged and inter-cooled) was rated at 175 hp. In this picture, Robert Wilberg of Osceola, Wisconsin, prepares a field for planting corn.

Bred for a better future

In the course of seven decades, tractor development has traveled very far indeed. When the pioneers talked proudly of ample power, it meant that they had managed to squeeze out 12 hp at the drawbar. When they spoke glowingly about the added versatility their latest innovation had brought, it referred to the fact that they had installed a second gear, giving the operator a choice of moving forward at a speed of 2¼ mph or 3 mph. When they praised the virtues of their new steering, it meant that they had replaced the chain construction with the type used on automobiles.

When today's John Deere salesman talks about ample power, he means 150 hp, or even 225 hp. When he says that the operator can travel at virtually any speed, he means that there are sixteen gears from which to choose. When he says that the steering has been improved, he means that the new model is equipped with variable-ratio hydrostatic power steering. It makes you wonder what the John Deere of the future will be like.

The photograph on this spread illustrates poignantly what the advancements in tractor development have meant to the farmer. What it took eight hours to do yesterday, today's operator can accomplish in one, thanks to the power and speed of the tractor and the size of the implement. Here, a 1985 4850 model with close to 200 hp lurking under the hood advances across a field of parsley on the Domingos Farms in the Salinas Valley, California.

Pictured above, a 2440 utility-type tractor performs its duties during the walnut harvest in California's San Joaquin Valley. The 2040 was brought out in 1975, and shows the new styling incorporated into the fifth generation of tractors. This new look was introduced in 1972. Such features as power steering, hydraulic brakes and planetary final drive were standard even on these smaller tractors. The 2440 produced 60 hp, measured at the PTO.

To the right, early morning in one of California's fertile valleys. Against the backdrop of sunlit golden hills, a 4630 speeds across a green field of beans, ripe for harvest, the tractor's implement cutting the plants just above the roots. The 4630, introduced in 1972, was the most powerful Deere of its time, not counting the four-wheel-drive versions. Its PTO power was rated at 150 hp. These new tractors had the Sound-Gard body and a choice of Syncro-Range, Quad-Range and Power Shift transmissions.

Today's Deere catalog includes a line of eight utility-type tractors, ranging from the 14 hp Model 650, to the 60 hp Model 1650. This photograph shows an example of the top-of-the-line model, decoratively parked in front of a stack of haybales on a farm in Patterson, California. The model is powered by a 190 ci four-cylinder engine, which has been turbocharged for increased efficiency. The transmission features nine forward speeds and three reverse. Four-wheel drive is a factory-installed option.

Next page
The photograph on these pages shows yet another example of the incredible range of tractors featured in the latest Deere catalog. The heavy-weight category of the 50-series is represented by a group of five tractors. Model 4850, captured here as it traverses one of the endless fields of California's fertile Salinas Valley, is the undisputed champion. Its turbocharged, intercooled six-cylinder engine produces 190 hp, and its Power Shift transmission gives the operator a choice of fifteen speeds.

Featured on these pages is the John Deere giant. This was the ultimate development of the four-wheel-drive tractor introduced in 1959 with the 8010. The redesigned and restyled 7020 and 7520 models came in 1971 and 1972, respectively. They were fitted with the new Roll-Gard cab, which could be had with both heater and air conditioning. There were two 78 gallon fuel tanks on board, and equipment could be attached without the operator leaving his seat.

In 1974 came further development of these four-wheel-drive giants, the 8430 and the 8630, the latter shown at speed in these photographs from California's Salinas Valley. The improvements have been accomplished by close collaboration with the farmers whose needs they serve; they needed more and more power. In this, the largest, machine power is supplied by a six-cylinder, 619-cubic-inch unit that produces 225 hp, measured at the PTO.

Although Model 5820 is not a tractor in the conventional sense, being a self-propelled forage harvester, it is featured here as a representative of the wide variety of specialized equipment manufactured by John Deere. The vehicle is powered by a 619 ci six-cylinder diesel engine, producing 290 hp. Height to the spout cap is almost twelve feet. That's about as tall as the corn grows in California's San Joaquin Valley, where this example was photographed. By the way, this contraption goes "backward," with the driver facing the harvester unit.

Model 2750, here seen pulling a load of lettuce near Salinas, California, was designed to meet the special needs of vegetable growers. Slow speed, high clearance and superb traction, are the characteristics that count. The 2750 can move at a snail's pace—as slow as half a mile per hour, to be exact. And the four-wheel drive, coupled with the tall tires (46 inches at the rear, 38 inches up front) ensures ample traction in the most slippery conditions. In fact, this type of tractor is called a "mudder."

Monuments to a past not forgotten

The John Deere Company has been building tractors for almost seven decades. Their numbers are counted in the hundreds and hundreds of thousands. Where have all the tractors gone? Surprisingly, many are still serving their masters—a diehard breed. these iron horses. But most sit abandoned in the grass, hidden in thickets of young trees, sunken in mud, forgotten in fields, overgrown with flowers, consumed by rust, washed by rain, smelted by sun. . . .

It is a slow death, but somehow they never seem quite dead. In fact, they are not. They can be resurrected anytime. Maybe this is why their owners let them sit there season after season. Maybe they tell themselves, "Someday I'll get that old thing runnin' again." In the meantime, the old Deere just sits there, like a monument to a past not forgotten.

Gordon Nelson of Chisago City, Minnesota—the name of the place sounds so much like Chicago and a large city, but it is small, kind of in the middle of nowhere—makes his living restoring tractors. He has a very well equipped workshop with lathes and drills and vises. In the back of his shop, one can find this rusty GP from 1930, complete with beautiful steering wheel.

This D and its companions are part of the Deere cemetery on the Dufner farm in North Dakota. The rust is eating away at them, and the weeds are growing fast around them. Yet, after all these years, there are still places the elements have not reached. There are still patches of original paint: at the end of a tank, on the inside of a fender, on the side of a flywheel. And the always-present can, covering any opening where the water can run in, shows that the owner has plans for the future.

The horizon is so distant in South Dakota's Badlands, the sky so huge, that you wonder how the old Model B got there in the first place. Was it an abandoned project? An attempt at homesteading? Or was it the end of a journey? No matter, for there are no more slow-turning wheels now, no fast-spinning flywheel, no turned steering wheel, pulled levers, depressed pedals.

The battery was the only thing worth rescuing, it seems. That thought makes your eye wander across to the amperes gauge, where the needle, in spite of the missing battery, indicates a slight charge. One wonders why this face is intact while the others are not.

The owner of this styled Model B from just before the war remembers the Deere arriving on his family's farm when he was five years old. It was used for a long time. Then something big broke, and it was cheaper to tow it behind the barn, where it still sits today. With the pigsty so close by, excess matter seeps into the ground where the tractor rests, making the Minnesota summer grass grow very tall and very green.

Historically speaking, the width between rows was determined by how close the horse could be driven to the previous row. This set a standard. And this standard was used to determine the width between the wheels of early tractors, which could straddle just one row, with front and rear wheels using the same tracks. Then came the GP, with its tricycle concept, enabling the tractor to straddle two rows.